To Have & To Hold
Sick Bags

Tim Sumner

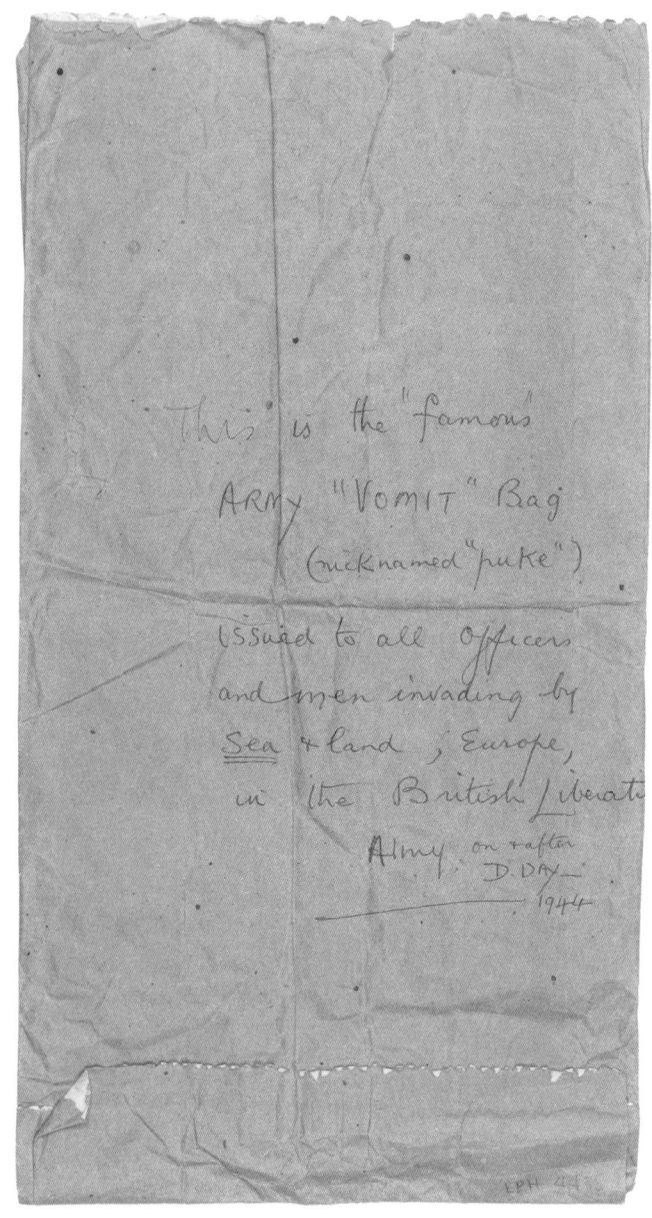

<<
United Airlines plane
over Manhattan, 1937

^
Army "Vomit" Bag
D–Day, France, 1944

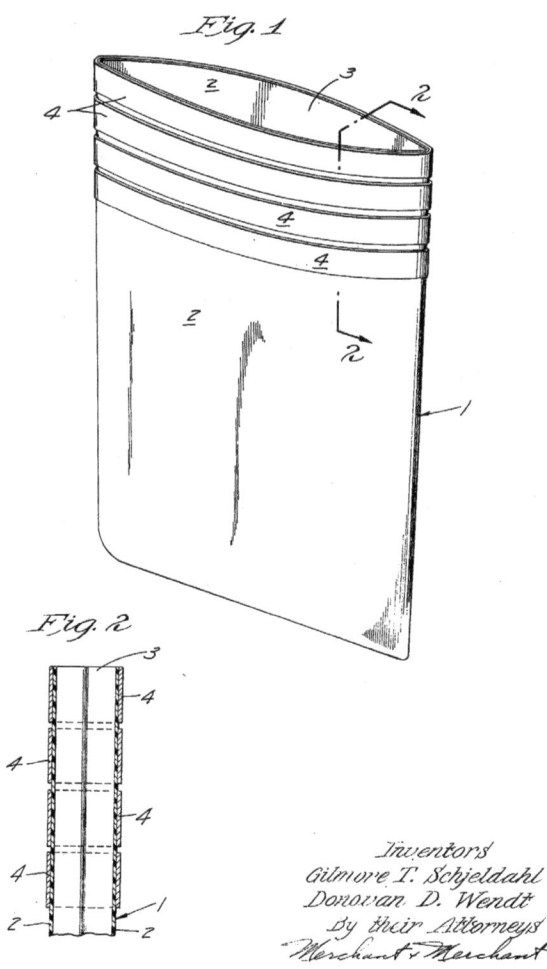

Gilmore T. Schjeldahl's patent for the airsickness bag, Nov. 7, 1949

AIR SICKNESS CURES DECLARED SIMPLE

Proper Ventilation of Cabins Usually Prevents Nausea, Survey Reveals.

ONLY 5% ARE SUFFERERS

Disorder Often is Psychological and Result of Nervousness, Guggenheim Fund Says.

One of the manifold problems connected with aviation with which the Daniel Guggenheim Fund for the Promotion of Aeronautics has concerned itself is air-sickness. The fund, which has fostered studies of the subject in the United States, Great Britain, Germany and Italy, issued yesterday a bulletin summarizing the results of the studies to date. The problem is characterized by Harry F. Guggenheim, president of the fund, as "a minor but difficult problem in passenger travel and one which, as yet, has not been entirely solved."

A solution, the bulletin states, would in all likelihood greatly increase the traffic by airplane.

"It is apparent that air-sickness is not only much less prevalent than seasickness," the bulletin says, "but is much more easily prevented or ameliorated by comparatively simple methods. Such statistics as are available indicate that only about five per cent of the passengers in air transportation are subject to air-sickness.

"In general, the difficulty is derived from two causes—one psychological, the other physical. Disorders of this kind are frequently the result of nervousness on the part of the individual who is not accustomed to aviation. The obvious solution here is, of course, the growing public confidence in aeronautical safety, and as airplane travel becomes more and more a matter of course, most of this psychological disorder will be eliminated.

"From the physical standpoint the particular cause of air-sickness seems to be lack of proper ventilation. Air-sickness occurs nearly always in closed cabin planes, and the successful passenger transport companies will be those which so design their cabins as to guarantee proper and adequate ventilation for their public.

"The general comfort of travel is also an important factor, and an efficient pilot who selects the proper air stratum and avoids bumpy riding, as far as possible, can do much to eliminate the risk of air-sickness for his passengers. It can be concluded that very few people are troubled by air-sickness in properly built, efficiently piloted aircraft."

Among the authorities quoted in the bulletin is the United States War Department, which distinguishes between ordinary air-sickness and so-called "altitude sickness," caused by the rarefication of the atmosphere at very high levels. In regard to sickness induced by ordinary flight, the department says in part:

"Why certain individuals show such susceptibility remains wholly unexplained. There is no reason for believing position in an airplane is especially provocative of headache, dizziness or nausea. In fact, it is less likely to provoke this symptomatology than is travel by sea. Happily, most individuals who become fearful, dizzy and nauseated on the edge of a high building, top of a tower or verge of a precipice experience no insecurity or discomfort in an airplane. The reason for this is that the rapid motion far removed from the broadly sketched map-like earth offers no downward perspective for altitude comparison."

ILLUSTRATORS GIVE DINNER.

Wallace Morgan, New President, Honored by Artists and Authors.

The Society of Illustrators gave a dinner last night at Hotel Brevoort in honor of its new president, Wallace Morgan. The dinner was attended by both the outgoing and incoming officers, as well as other illustrators and authors.

In time illustrators will feel the effect of the recent Wall Street crash, Harry Hirshfield, cartoonist asserted. Mr. Hirshfield said that he thought artists were becoming more interested in the technique of art and that as a consequence they were losing something of the romance which had always attached to them.

Other speakers were Wallace Irwin, Howard Chandler Christy, Wallace Morgan and Charles Dana Gibson. Rueben L. Goldberg presided. Tony Sarg showed a marionette.

Treaty With Portugal in Force.

Special to The New York Times.

WASHINGTON, Nov. 1.—The State Department announced today that the treaty of arbitration which was negotiated with Portugal last Spring has come into force with the exchange of ratifications by Joseph P. Cotton, Under Secretary of State, and Viscount D'Alte, the Portuguese Minister. The treaty is similar to a score of others entered into with various governments in the last two years.

LIGHT MEAL URGED FOR AIR TRAVELERS

Pre-Flight Prescription to Bar Motion Sickness Emphasizes Non-Greasy Food, No Alcohol

A light, non-greasy meal before flying and abstinence from alcohol were recommended yesterday for avoiding air sickness by Dr. Kenneth L. Stratton, director of American Airlines' medical division.

In a year's study of motion sickness Dr. Stratton found that although relatively few persons were affected, precautions were advisable. Among drugs to counteract nausea dramamine was reported to be effective.

Dr. Stratton likened motion sickness to the common cold in that the cause never had been pinned down to an ultimate source. He said that some authorities attributed it to "a confusion between the eyes and the body's stabilization mechanism," while others believed that abnormal motion, "such as the swaying of an automobile or the pitching of a ship at sea," affected the organs of balance.

Apprehension plays a large part in many cases, but the traveler's physical condition is perhaps a more important factor, Dr. Stratton declared.

"We made a survey last year to determine the effectiveness of dramamine in air travel," he related. "We tried the drug on 719 cases of persons with air sickness. They ranged in age from 5 years up and we gave them a standard dose of one tablet, or 100 milligrams. Better than 80 per cent of them enjoyed complete or partial relief.

"Our studies showed that 8 to 10 per cent of this group had mild side reactions, mostly drowsiness. We cut the dosage in half and found that the drug retained its curative power but lost all but an insignificant fraction of its side effects."

The physician reported that dramamine was standard equipment on all planes of American Airlines and American Overseas Airlines. Before the drug became generally available about a year ago the aircraft carried hyoscine and several forms of barbiturates as curatives. They were found unsatisfactory.

Dr. Stratton estimated that one air traveler in 200 was subject to air sickness. He indicated that it would occur less frequently because of newer pressurized-cabin planes that flew at altitudes where turbulence often was avoided.

Although the drowsiness or dizziness caused by dramamine is slight, Dr. Stratton said, persons using it should not drive an automobile or fly a plane immediately afterward.

'I don't think there is anything wrong with white space. I don't think it's a problem to have a blank wall.'

^ Annie Leibovitz

<<

The New York Times
Nov 2, 1929 / May 23, 1950

^

Steven with examples from
his archive of 3600 sick bags

A Patron of Puke

By Steven Silberberg

Annie Leibovitz surely does not collect air sickness bags. The bane of those of us who do collect barf bags is the plain white blank bag that is void of any printing whatsoever.

Airlines largely no longer print instructions, logos or messages on their motion sickness bags, much less whimsical copy / art as they once did in their heyday. After all, it costs money to print text and images on these bags – and even more in colour – not to mention the expense of hiring a designer.

In fact, even providing enough plain white bags for every passenger costs more than you'd expect. Sure, the bags themselves are relatively inexpensive. But passengers also use them as scratch pads or as a writing surface. Enough scribbling on a sick bag and the cleaning crew must replace these bags, which in turn increases costs.

That's why some carriers (looking at you, United) now foil would be scribes with dark blue bags. The printing costs are initially high, but given the rarity of motion sickness these days, the bags can remain in the seat back almost indefinitely. Who knows? You might find year old trash in one of those bags on your next flight.

Despite the dearth of design and paucity of originality in modern air sickness bags, there was a time when each item in an airplane reflected the branding and sensibilities of the carrier. Icelandair and Skyways (Swedish) are among several whose bags once featured a pretty flower. Elegant design is common among Scandinavian airlines.

Considering the intended use of air sickness bags, it would seem a bit absurd to collect them. But I find it interesting to see how the attitudes of airlines and even countries are reflected in their designs.

Air sickness bag collectors are a small, tight-knit niche community, probably not too shockingly. But a surprising number of airline passengers will on occasion grab a bag as a souvenir of their trip. Eventually, when cleaning out their junk drawers, these collectors sometimes seek out my website and offer to send me the souvenir they took from their early 80s trip to the Orient or whatever, that they just can't throw out. I lovingly refer to these people (or anybody whom I swap spare bags with for that matter) as Patrons of Puke.

Sick bag collecting also helps me keep my depression-era scarcity weltanschauung in check. As someone with a predilection towards hoarding, I find that channelling this compulsion into a single collection makes it far easier avoid the irrational desire to hold on to everything and anything. I only care about collecting bags and can let go of everything else.

Before sick bags, it all started with numismatics and philately since those are the items that were readily available to a child in the late 60s. Soon, I ditched those and started collecting pennants from sports teams and tourist destinations, which have a lot more character than coins and stamps and make far better display pieces.

But as I got older, my sensibilities changed. It occurred to me that collecting items which were never meant to be collected might be interesting. What would it be like to have the world's largest collection of sardine keys for example?

I was going to find out in earnest. After collecting a few dozen sardine keys, I realized that not only were they challenging to obtain they were even more challenging to distinguish from one another. Sure, even someone with severe myopia can discern slight differences between a King Oscar sardine key and an Underwood sardine key, but it's not easy or particularly gratifying. And you can't just look at the minor variations and remember which is which.

Then in college in 1982, I was on a long, empty United flight from Boston to San Francisco. I looked in the seat back and the proverbial light shone out at me just like in the movies. "Resolved that I will be an air sickness bag collector! I'm sure nobody else collects these." I was wrong, of course, but that's where it all began.

But then, if you don't travel internationally for business (or even vacation) how do you grow your collection? Sure, friends and relatives return from flights with the latest new bags and are happy to help, but growing the collection significantly requires leverage.

As someone with a programming background, I figured that the World Wide Web would be the perfect venue for displaying my collection. So in 1997, I secured the domains airsicknessbags.com, barfbags.com and sickbags.com and built a website that displayed all the bags – probably between 100-200 of them.

Now people anywhere could find me and donate in exchange for attribution and/or a spare bag. Even as the World Wide Web was a newfangled curiosity, like-minded people found the site.

Possibly not as entertaining as the Hamster Dance, but you could waste a lot more time at the Air Sickness Bag Museum.

As the collection has grown, so has the website. Bags and patrons are now all part of a relational database that helps in searching and cataloguing. This would probably be mind numbingly agonizing for the average chronicler of anything, but for a programmer it's actually a nice bonus of collecting. A frustrating bonus when there are coding issues, but still satisfying.

However, lest you think I collect sick bags out of some obsessive anthropological curiosity or sociological research, I just think it's fun. Even 3600 bags in, I still delight at seeing a new design from an airline I didn't even know existed.

Collecting barf bags can even act as social lubrication. Not that anyone would introduce themselves as a collector of motion sickness bags, but once people find out about the collection they enjoy being in on the joke, and often have insightful questions and historical tidbits or personal experiences to relate.

Not surprisingly, there are some people who are bewildered by the hobby and even exhibit mild disdain because of the disgusting function of the collectible. People have noticeably distanced themselves from me on some occasions when they learned of the pastime.

It turns out that this self-selection is a good litmus test for the sensibilities of who I might ultimately get along with. So – a social time-saver (as if I have some dumb need to save time in my social life).

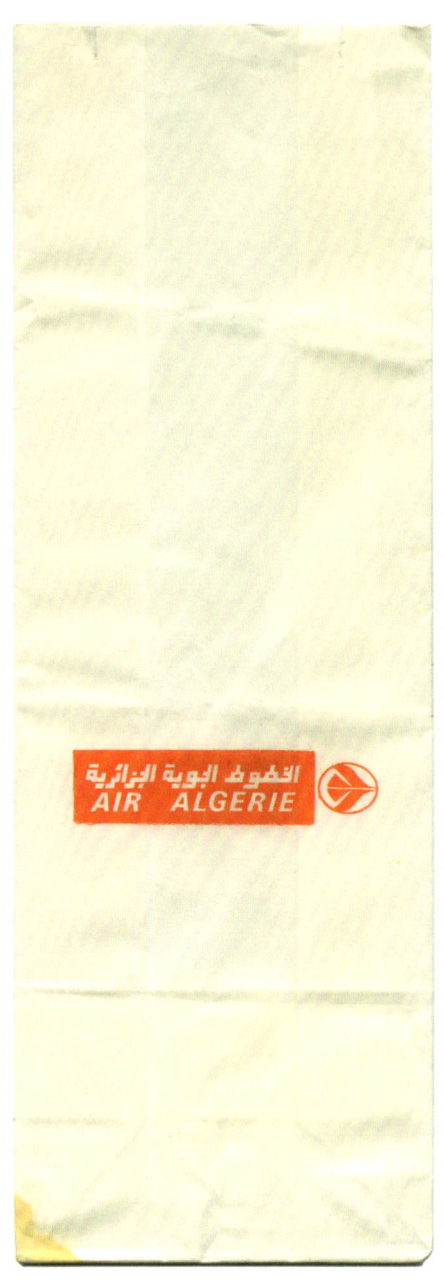

feeling **unwell?**
E mauiui ana ahau
braak 吐物
erbrechen
kräkas vómito
嘔吐 *vomi*

how ever you say it
it all comes out the same

If affected by motion sickness, use this bag and not your carry on

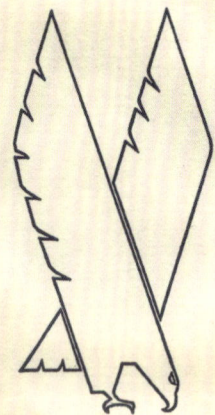

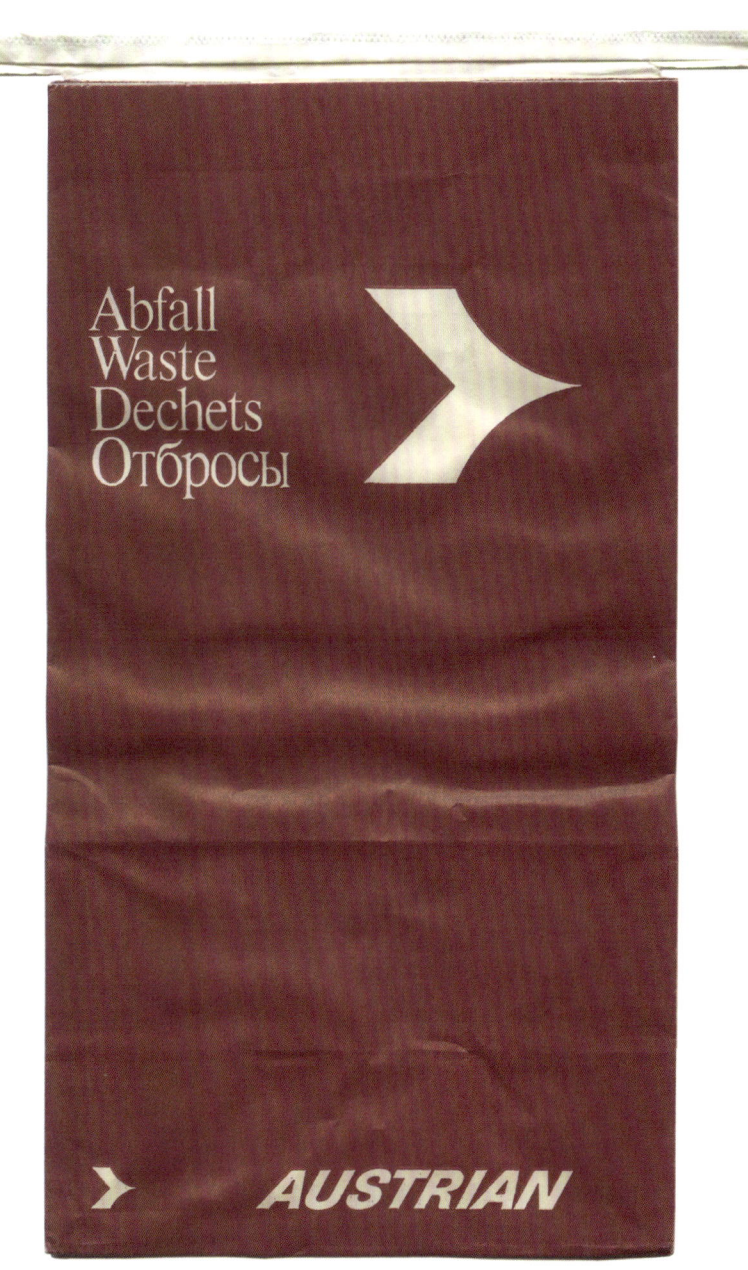

**After use please call
Stewardess for disposal**

Cyprus Airways

**AIRSICKNESSBAG
SAC POUR MAL DE L'AIR**

IN THE EVENT OF SICKNESS
PLEASE CALL CABIN CREW
FOR ASSISTANCE

TEAR OFF TO OPEN
ここを引きはがし

WATERPROOF DISPOSAL BAG
（防水加工をされています）

携帯入れにご利用下さい。

JAPAN AIR LINES

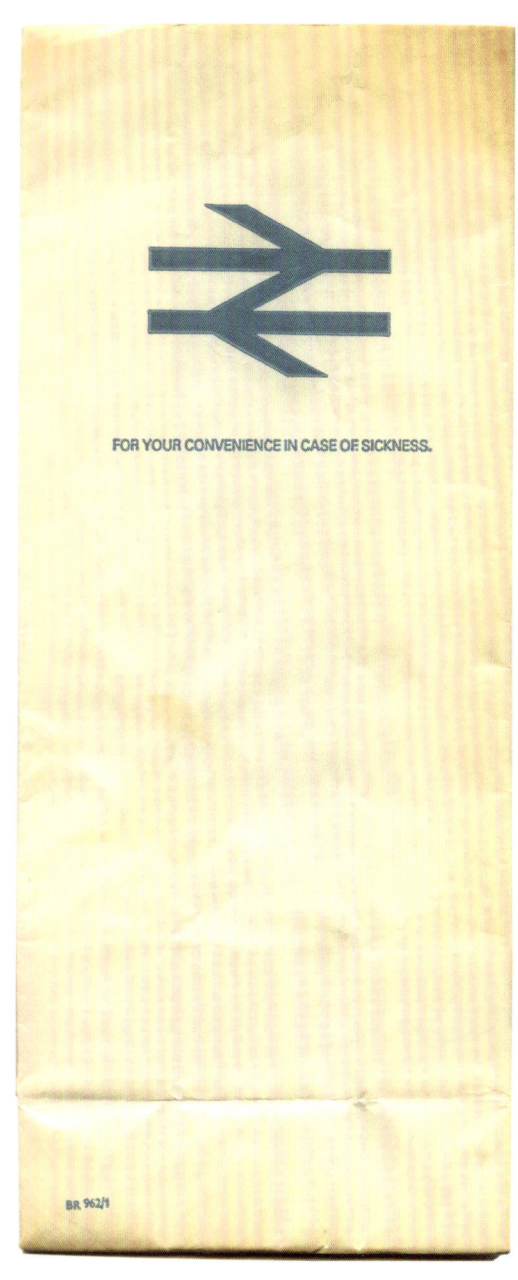

"In a while you will be fine"-bag

FOR MOTION DISCOMFORT

PAL

Tear off to open ⬆ لفتح الكيس أقطع من هنا

OTHER USES FOR A SICK BAG

No. 4 in a series of 25.

DOGGY BAG

Why leave that lamb chop on the plate after that executive lunch?
 Simply put it in this bag, seal it and cook it up later. Mmmm... Can't you just taste it?
 Your colleagues will marvel at your ingenuity. Your clients will be impressed with your improvisation.
 It couldn't be easier!
 The doggy bag is a real must for every man on the move!

THIS SUGGESTION WAS BROUGHT TO YOU COURTESY OF
STEMETIL EFF
PRESCRIPTION MEDICINE PROCHLORPERAZINE

OTHER USES FOR A SICK BAG

No. 13 in a series of 25.

FOOD BLENDER

Who needs a food processor?!

Say goodbye to washing up mixing bowls.

Now you can blend your food the easy way.

Just put your fruit or vegetables in this bag, seal the top, place on the floor and stamp away!

Mashed potatoes have never been so mashed!

You can hear them say: "HEY, MUM! NO LUMPS!!!!"

And after the meal? Just throw the bag away. No mess. No fuss. No washing up.

You can even eat straight from the bag!

THIS SUGGESTION WAS BROUGHT TO YOU COURTESY OF

STEMETIL EFF
PRESCRIPTION MEDICINE PROCHLORPERAZINE

vueling

WE LOVE PLACES

WE

YOU TO THE MOON AND BAG

Usa esta bolsa en caso de mareo y avísanos.
Use this bag if you feel sick and let us know.
Usa questo sacchetto in caso di nausea e avvisaci.

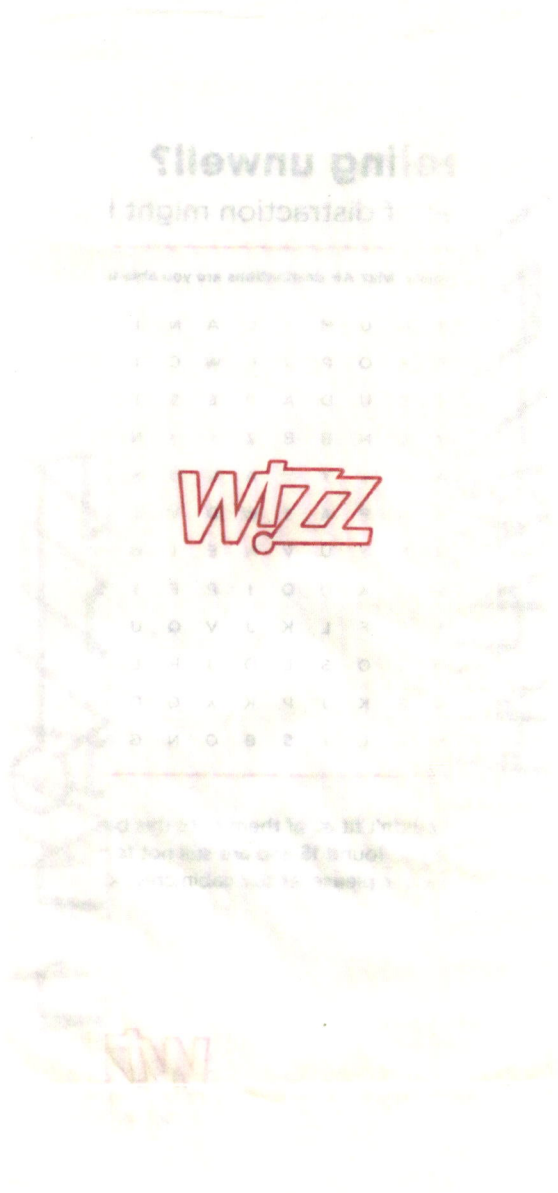

Feeling unwell?
A bit of distraction might help.

How many Wizz Air destinations are you able to spot?

V	T	N	U	M	I	L	A	N	I	E	P
I	S	K	O	P	J	E	W	C	I	I	A
E	T	B	U	D	A	P	E	S	T	T	O
N	M	E	N	B	B	Z	I	J	N	T	C
N	W	D	L	Y	V	A	V	O	S	E	F
A	A	N	P	A	T	W	D	V	I	N	M
M	R	N	Y	U	V	N	E	I	B	E	O
H	S	I	K	U	O	I	P	F	I	R	S
D	A	R	F	L	K	J	V	Q	U	I	C
D	W	I	O	S	L	O	J	H	L	F	O
V	B	G	K	J	P	K	X	G	D	E	W
T	M	A	L	I	S	B	O	N	G	L	I

We couldn't fit all of them onto this bag. But if you found **15** and are still not feeling any better, please let our cabin crew know.

wizzair.com

Index

To Have & To Hold

3 Sick Bags

446-500

Thanks
Jodi Leach
Andy Bainbridge
James Fishlock
Matt Taylor
Justin Hobson
David Longfield
Margaret Schuelein
Steven Silberberg

Image Credits:

Page 04–05
© Mary Evans / Everett Collection

Page 06
© IWM EPH 4435

Page 08–09
© The New York Times

To Have & To Hold
Issue Number 3 – Sick Bags

Tim Sumner / SUMNER.WORKS

First edition 2023
Published and distributed by SUMNER.WORKS

ISBN: 978-1-8381845-3-7

SUMNER.WORKS © 2023

SUMNER.WORKS

PAPERBAGARCHIVE.COM

Edition of 500 / Hand Numbered

Print
Print love Ltd / Yorkshire / UK

Typeface
Söhne / Klim Type Foundry / New Zealand

Stock
Offenbach Bible / 80GSM / Fenner Paper
Sixties / 60GSM / Fenner Paper

Every effort has been made to contact the rights holders of the material reproduced. In most cases we've received permission and in others had no response, or we've not been able to contact the rights owners.

The publisher will happily rectify this in future editions. We hope all rights holders accept that these bags are reproduced in a spirit of celebration and admiration.